ENCOURAGING MYSELF:

MY EXPERIENCES AND

SCRIPTURES GOD GAVE TO ME

Rebecca Gaskins-Mejia

Copyright Page

© 2022 Rebecca Gaskins-Mejia
**Encouraging Myself:
My Experiences and Scriptures
God Gave to Me**

First Printing

All rights reserved. Reproduction in whole or part without written permission from the publisher or author is strictly prohibited. Printed in the United States of America.

This book is inspired by the Holy Spirit, Who teaches us all things.

All Scripture is taken from several versions of the Holy Bible, public domain

Rebecca Gaskins-Mejia
Myrtle Beach, South Carolina

Simply This Publishing

Kindle Direct Publishing

Cover picture © witsanu/Adobe Stock
Frame picture © Elena/Adobe Stock

ENCOURAGING MYSELF

ENCOURAGING MYSELF

Introduction

God bless you. My name is Rebecca Gaskins - Mejia. The Lord put it on my heart to share some of my life experiences. We can go through life without anyone there to encourage us as we face and go through trials. So, I wrote this little devotional book to help someone who may be experiencing some of the struggles and challenges I had to face on this journey with our Lord and Savior Jesus Christ.

I pray and thank God to be a testimony for others and to share some of my stories and experiences on how he taught me the way to encourage myself.

I hope and pray by the blessing of the Lord as you read this little book of devotional encouragement for yourself that you may know God saw me through it all and He will do the same for you. He's the same God today as He was yesterday.

ENCOURAGING MYSELF

Trusting God

Chapter One

When I deal with everyday life; it seems like I don't know what to do. It feels like I can't move forward, or I feel like I'm at a stand still. But knowing that God is there and he's able to reassure me of things in my life. Trusting God is not an easy task. Being able to let go or release certain things to God for me was kind of challenging; I had to know within myself, no matter how I felt, thought and or saw things. For me, trusting was a learning experience and it still is.

And now, Lord, what wait I for? My hope is in thee.

(Psalm 39:7)

Hope thou in God: for I shall yet praise him, who is the health of my countenance and my God.

(Psalm 42:11)

*The Lord of host is with us; the God of Jacob
is our refuge.*

(Psalm 46:7)

*Be still and know that I am God: I will be
exalted among the heathen. I will be exalted
in the earth.*

(Psalm 46:10)

*Because of his strength will I wait upon thee:
for God is my defence.*

(Psalm 59:9)

*My soul fainteth for thy salvation: but I hope
in thy word.*

(Psalm 71:14)

*Thou art my hiding place and my shield: I
hope in thy word.*

(Psalm 119:114)

*Blessed is the man that trusteth in the Lord,
and whose hope in the Lord is.*

(Jeremiah 17:7)

*The Lord is my portion, saith my soul:
therefore will I hope in him.*

*The Lord is good unto them that wait for him
to the soul that seeketh him.*

*It is good that man should both hope and
quietly wait for the salvation of the Lord.*

(Lamentations 3:24-26)

Be not afraid, only believe.

(Mark 5:36)

*And not only so but we glory in tribulation
also, knowing that tribulation worketh
patience; And patience, experience; and
experience, hope: And hope maketh not
ashamed.*

(Romans 5:3-5)

*Now faith is the substance of things hoped
for, the evidence of things not seen.*

(Hebrews 11:1)

And every man that hath this hope in him purifieth himself, even as he is pure.

(1 John 3:3)

*"God, my dear heavenly Father; empty
me out of myself so I can fully
trust you.
Amen"*

ENCOURAGING MYSELF

Rest

Chapter Two

Resting and waiting on the Lord is not an easy thing to do. Sometimes I feel like I can't go left, right, front or back. I'm at a stand still praying, wishing and hoping that the Lord Jesus Christ will give me a sign on which direction to go. Also, I know the promises He told me, but the pain of resting and waiting is learning to stay focused. He only asks me to depend on him; to rest patiently.

I will both lay me down in peace, and sleep:
for thou, Lord, only makest me dwell
in safety.

(Psalm 4:8)

Rest in the Lord, and wait patiently for him:
fret not thyself because of him who
prospereth in his way, because of the man
who bringeth wicked devices to pass.

(Psalm 37:7)

He that dewelleth in the secret place of the most High shall abide under the shadow of the Almighty.

(Psalm 91:1)

When thou liest down, thou shalt not be afraid: yea; thou shalt lie down, and thy sleep shall be sweet.

(Proverbs 3:24)

Again and again, I've found Him faithful to respond, and the closer I move to Him, the safer I feel and the better I rest.

*"Lord Jesus,
Keep my heart and eyes fixed upon
you; so I can get through these fiery
trials of learning how to rest and
wait upon you.
Amen."*

Patience

Chapter Three

I didn't understand why things weren't moving in my life. I wanted things done quickly. But I seemed to struggle with being patient. Waiting on God seemed like years. My heart and spirit seemed at the time to get restless. But, I learned by holding fast because no matter what, it is better than giving up.

And let us not be weary in well doing: for in due season we shall reap, if we faint not.

(Galatians 6:9)

For ye have need of patience, that after ye have done the will of God, ye might receive the promise.

(Hebrews 10:36)

And let us run with patience the race that is set before us.

(Hebrews 12:1)

And the Lord direct your hearts into the love of God, and into patience waiting for Christ.

(2 Thessalonians 3:5)

Knowing this, that the trying of our faith worketh patience.

But let patience have her prefect work, that ye may be prefect and entire, wanting nothing.

(James 1:3-4)

Be ye also patience, stablish your hearts: for the coming of the Lord draweth nigh.

(James 5:8)

But if, when ye do well, and suffer for it, ye take it patiently, this is acceptable with God.

(1 Peter 2:20)

"Lord,
Sometimes I look for a sign. I feel like I
need directions, and I need it now!
Lord, give me patience. Give me faith.
Instead of seeking a sign, let me live
expectantly for every day miracles and
listen for your still small voice.
Amen."

Believe

Chapter Four

When so many trials hit my life; I really didn't know where I stood. It felt like the cares of this world were weighing me down, when I tried moving forward. But what is there more to do; I thought to myself. I try and hope for the best of everything; even when I didn't understand it.

The Lord is a refuge for the oppressed, a stronghold in time of trouble.

(Psalm 9:9)

Therefore I say unto you, what things soever ye desire, when you pray, believe that ye receive them, and ye shall have them.

(Psalm 11:24)

The Lord is my light and my salvation; whom shall I fear? the Lord is the strength of my life; of whom shall I be afraid?

(Psalm 27:1)

The Lord is my strength and my shield; my heart trusted in him, and I am helped: therefore my heart greatly rejoiceth; and with my song will I praise him.

(Psalm 28:7)

Those who seek the Lord lack no good thing.

(Psalm 34:10)

God is our refuge and strength, a very present help in trouble.

(Psalm 46:1)

Surely he shall no be moved for ever: the righteous shall be in everlasting remembrance.

He shall not be afraid of evil tiding: his heart is fixed, trusting in the Lord.

(Psalm 112:6-7)

Thou will keep him in perfect peace, whose mind is stayed on thee:

Trust ye in the Lord forever: for in the Lord JEHOVAH is everlasting strength.

(Isaiah 26:3-4)

And all things, whatsoever ye ask in prayer, believing, ye shall receive.

(Matthew 21:22)

Let not your heart be troubled; believe in God, believe also in me.

(John 14:1)

But my God shall supply all my needs according to HIS riches in glory by Christ Jesus.

(Ephesians 4:19)

Finally my brethren, be strong in the Lord, and in the power of his might.

(Ephesians 6:10)

I can do all things through Christ which strengtheneth me.

(Philippians 4:13)

My brethren, count it all joy when ye fall into divers temptation,

Knowing this, that the trying of your faith worketh patience.

But let patience have her perfect work, that ye may be prefect and entire, wanting nothing.

(James 1:2-4)

"Father,
Help me to keep believing, to push
forward even though I feel restless and
weak. Keep my eyes and heart
steadfast on the promises you told me
that I can have because of you.
Amen"

Faith

Chapter Five

As I go through challenges and suffering. Faith is there even when I don't see it but I keep walking, pushing, standing, and persevering in all things. No matter what's going on around me. I don't ever stop moving or believing in a request that I made to my Lord Jesus Christ and Savior.

The Lord is my shepherd and I shall not want.

(Psalm 23:1)

Cast thy burden upon the Lord, and he shall sustain thee: he shall never suffer the righteous to be moved.

(Psalm 55:22)

I will lift up my eyes unto the hills, from whence cometh my help.

My help cometh from the Lord, which made heaven and earth.

(Psalm 121:1-2)

No weapon formed against thee shall prosper; and every tongue that shall rise against thee in judgment thou shalt condemn.

(Isaiah 54:17)

And the Lord said, If ye had faith as a grain of mustard seed, ye shall say unto this mountain, Remove hence to yonder place, and it shall remove and nothing shall be impossible unto you.

(Matthew 17:20)

Be not afraid, only believe.

(Mark 5:36)

Jesus said unto him, If thou canst believe, all things are possible to him that believe.

(Mark 9:23)

And Jesus answering saith unto them, Have faith in God.

For verily I say unto you, That whosoever shall say unto this mountain, Be thou removed, and be thou cast into the sea; and shall not doubt in his heart, but shall believe that those things which he saith shall come to pass; he shall have whatsoever he saith.

(Mark 11:22-23)

For we walk by faith and not by sight.

(2 Corinthians 5:7)

And let us not be weary in well doing: for in due season we shall reap if we faint not.

(Galatians 6:9)

I can do all things through Christ which strengthens me.

(Philippians 4:13)

*But my God shall supply all my needs,
according to His riches and glory in
Christ Jesus.*

(Philippians 4:19)

*Now faith is the substance of things hoped
for, the evidence of things not seen.*

(Hebrews 11:1)

*But let him ask in faith, nothing wavering.
For he that wavereth is like a wave of the sea
driven with wind and tossed.*

(Hebrews 11:6)

"Father,
Please, help me to be the person of faith
you called me to be; now believing that
you will work all details out in my life.
Let me not rely on tangible,
explainable things, but to remember
that YOU are in control of everything
known and unknown. Father, increase
my faith in you the more; as I trust you
and walk without seeing
or knowing.
Amen."

Obedience

Chapter Six

Experiencing obedience is not easy. I know, I had to learn by giving up things in order to gain in the plan of God for my life. Being disobedient brings on hurt, pain, and suffering by not letting go of my own selfish ways and will. But the more I submit to disobedience; I'm denying myself to learn how to trust, rest, believe and have faith. I know now these are the keys to understanding the obedience needed in my life.

Now therefore, if ye will obey my voice indeed, and keep my covenant, then ye shall be a peculiar treasure unto me above all people: for the earth is mine.

(Exodus 19:5)

Keep therefore the words of this covenant, and do them, that ye may prosper in all that ye do.

(Deuteronomy 29:9)

I command thee this day to love the Lord thy God, to walk in his ways and to keep his commandments and his statutes and his judgments, that thou mayest live and multiply: and the Lord thy God shall bless thee in the land whither thou goest to possess it.

(Deuteronomy 30:16)

*And Samuel said, Hath the L*ORD *as great delight in burnt offerings and sacrifices, as in obeying the voice of the L*ORD*? Behold, to obey is better than sacrifice, and to hearken than the fat of rams.*

(1 Samuel 15:22)

If they obey and serve him, they shall spend their days in prosperity, and their years in pleasure.

(Job 36:11)

All the paths of the Lord are mercy and truth unto such as keep his covenant and his testimonies.

(Psalm 25:10)

*Blessed are they that keep his testimonies,
and that seek him with their whole heart.*

(Psalm 119:2)

*My son forget not my law; but let thine heart
keep my commandments:*

*For length of days, and long life, and peace.
Shall they add
to thee.*

(Proverbs 3:1-2)

*If you be willing and obedient, ye shall eat the
good of the land.*

(Isaiah 1:19)

*Not everyone that saith Lord, Lord, shall
enter into the kingdom of heaven; but he that
doeth the will of my Father which is in
heaven.*

(Matthew 7:21)

*But he said, Yea rather, blessed are they that
hear the word of God, and keep it.*

(Luke 11:28)

But whoso looketh into the perfect law of liberty, and continueth therein, he being not a forgetful hearer, but a doer of the work, this man shall be blessed in his deed.

(James 1:25)

*"Father,
The oath of life is often a difficult
struggle. I ask not that You make it
smooth or easy, but to illustrate it so
that I can see to walk in total
obedience. Even for a moment, if the
light is dim, help me walk by faith,
trusting You with each step I will take.
For your ways are righteous
and perfect.
Amen."*

ENCOURAGING MYSELF

The End

Praise God you have read to the end of this little book of devotionals. I pray that it will help or enlighten your sense of assurance, that you are who God says you are in Him. Also, then to be able to encourage yourself if nobody else does.

Furthermore, knowing that we sometimes expect encouragement from others but that doesn't always happen. We mostly need to learn to encourage oneself and recognizing one's accomplishments and goals through Christ Jesus who is our source and strength.

Once again, I say thank you and God bless you for picking this little book to encourage your heart in the Lord; as He did for me, He will do for you; this being good while able to share these little pieces of my experiment from my own life.

ENCOURAGING MYSELF

Acknowledgements

I want to give praise, honor, glory and thanks to my Lord and Savior Jesus Christ, who inspired my heart to write this little devotional book. To be able to encourage others on what He can do when you allow Him to work through you.

Also, my heart, my joy, and my blessing by God giving me my children: Angelic C.T. Gaskins, Manish C.R. Gaskins, Sa'-rai O. J. Mejia and Samuel J. Mejia. And furthermore, being blessed with four beautiful grandchildren: Raven, Braylen, Angelus, and Azaylee.

And furthermore, my Spiritual Godmother Bridget B. S. Thomas: Her tough love, whipple-ball stick corrections with thus said the Lord and her push for me to move forward in the Lord and the things for the Kingdom of God.

Love,
Sister Happy
(Rebecca)

AUTHOR PAGE

Rebecca Gaskins-Mejia

My name is Rebecca Gaskins Mejia. I'm from Horry County but I grew up in a small little town there called Toddsville, South Carolina. I am a mother with two sons, two daughters and four grandchildren. I gave my life to Christ December the 17th, 1995. Through the years I was an Usher, on the Pastor's Aide Committee, Armour-bearer, part of the youth group and Nurses Aid for the Pastor with the church I attended for 13 years until God transitioned me. I am also involved with a soup kitchen which feeds many needy people and I have been there for 5 years now and been on a Radio Gospel Station for 2 years also. I love getting involved with things concerning the Kingdom of God. I love to worship, pray and to spend time with God.